the TEN COMMANDMENTS *for* MANAGERS

GREG BLENCOE

The Ten Commandments for Managers
Copyright © 2004 by Greg Blencoe

ISBN 0-9675893-2-0

Published by August Publishing
Manufactured in the United States of America

Book cover and interior design by:
Irene Archer, www.book-cover-design.com

First Edition

THE TEN COMMANDMENTS FOR MANAGERS

INTRODUCTION

The ultimate goal of an effective manager is to recruit and develop a group of highly productive employees and work with them to fulfill organizational objectives. The question is: What steps need to be taken to achieve that outcome? *The Ten Commandments for Managers* was written to answer that question.

The big secret to managing employees is that there is no big secret to managing employees. The steps that managers need to take to do their job well fall into the realm of what most people consider to be common sense. But the discipline to execute these common sense principles on a consistent basis is what makes the manager's job so difficult.

The cold truth is that there are no short cuts to being a successful manager. You have to commit to being good and make a daily habit of putting these principles into practice. Managing employees is like anything in life, you get out of it what you put into it.

Because most managers probably don't want to spend their free time reading management books, this book was written so it can be comfortably read in one sitting. It is not intended to cover every situation that you will face as a manager, but it will give you a foundation that you will be able to apply to your own situation.

Without further ado, here are *The Ten Commandments for Managers...*

COMMANDMENT I

SURROUND YOURSELF WITH HIGH QUALITY EMPLOYEES

"No matter how good or successful you are or how clever or crafty, your business and its future are in the hands of the people you hire." [1]

—Akio Morita
Co-founder and former CEO, Sony

Managers must delegate tasks and responsibilities because one person can only do so much. The question is: To whom will you be delegating? Will you be delegating to someone who is hardworking or lazy, polite or rude, organized or unorganized, competent or inept, talented or not talented?

Hire the Best Employee for the Job

For a product to succeed, customers demand that it be consistently excellent. At the end of the day, the quality of your product is largely going to determine the success of your business, and your employees play a major role in determining that level of quality. An ironclad principle of business is that if you tolerate mediocre employees, then you tolerate giving your customers a mediocre product. It is unacceptable to have an "OK" or "decent" or "so-so" group of employees unless you find it acceptable to give your customers an "OK" or "decent" or "so-so" product. Therefore, you should figure out exactly what you want in an employee and then be relentless in your pursuit of somebody who is as close to that ideal as possible.

The extra cost and effort needed to find and attract the right person for the job is actually little compared to all of the indirect expenses that will accrue as a result of having a mediocre employee. What is the cost if an employee can't get along with others? What is the cost if an employee does not show up to work on a consistent basis? What is the cost if an employee does not treat customers well? What is the cost if the employee makes mistakes all the time? What is the cost if an employee quits soon after he is hired? Therefore, you can either invest a little more time and money upfront for the right employee or pay a lot later for the wrong one.

Herb Kelleher, the legendary former CEO of Southwest Airlines, discusses a situation he faced that gives some insight into his attitude about finding the right employee:

"Some years ago our vice president of the people department told me the department had interviewed 34 people for a ramp agent position in Amarillo, Texas, and she was a little embarrassed about the amount of time it was taking

and the implied cost of it, and my answer was, 'If you have to interview 134 people to get the right attitude on the ramp in Amarillo, Texas, do it.'[2]

Finding High Quality Employees

The first step in hiring is to come up with a job description. The job description serves as the basis for determining exactly what you are looking for in a candidate. It should explain why the job exists and what job functions are regularly performed in the position. You should determine the requirements for the position in terms of education, job experience, skills, and personality traits. Then, prioritize the requirements starting with what is absolutely necessary.

If you have not been closely involved in that particular job, you will want to pick the brain of one of your employees who does have experience in that area. This will help you determine the skills needed to excel in the position. You should also make sure the job description is up to date, because some jobs evolve over time.

The job description can be a very valuable tool in advertising and interviewing for the position. If it accurately portrays the position, the job description can tell candidates exactly what they will be doing if they get the job. This will allow candidates to rule themselves out if it is clear they are not what you are looking for. In addition, when going through resumes or applications, you can use the list of requirements to weed out unqualified candidates.

Once you have a clear job description and a clear idea of what you are looking for, you can begin searching for qualified candidates. The question often comes up: Where do I look to find high quality employees? The short answer is: everywhere. There are numerous ways to find potential employees. For example, they can be found through:

◆ Headhunters

◆ Temp agencies

◆ The company website

◆ Bulletin boards around the office

◆ Networking groups

◆ The local high school or college

◆ Your church

◆ Businesses where you are a customer

◆ Customers of your business

◆ Newspaper ads

◆ Groups with retirees who may consider part-time work

◆ Employment websites such as Monster.com

◆ "Help Wanted" signs you put up at a retail location

◆ Communication with former high quality employees who left on good terms and may want to come back after realizing the grass isn't greener on the other side

◆ Previous jobs you have held

◆ Chamber of commerce meetings

The key is to always be on the lookout for potential employees who would do well working for you. For example, Nucor Corporation employs a highly productive workforce and is the largest steel producer in the United States. One way they find good employees is to observe the construction workers when a new plant is being built. The best ones are recruited to stay on once the plant is functioning.[3]

When hiring for a position, you should give the people inside your organization a fair chance to get the job. Promoting from within is a good policy if the candidate is qualified. This increases morale because employees realize there are opportunities for advancement. If outsiders are always hired, your current employees may begin to think that they will always be stuck in their current position no matter how well they perform. Also, current employees know how the company operates so the learning process will be easier. In addition, this acquisition method is cheaper for you since you don't have to apply as many resources to locating and interviewing outside candidates. However, this does not mean that you should hire unqualified candidates just because they work inside the company.

Your current employees can also be very valuable recruiters. If they are working with other good employees, being treated fairly and with respect, receiving appreciation for good work, and having their ideas, opinions, and concerns heard, then they will speak positively about their experiences with the company. Soon, you will be flooded with job applicants. Remember, winners want to be surrounded by winners and play on a winning team.

One of the advantages of getting employees through referrals is that the new hires will have a good chance of being successful and staying longer than the ones who are not referred to the company. The current employee can give them a crystal clear picture of what it is like to work for the company. This allows potential employees to decide whether or not they can function well in that environment. New employees who do not have the inside scoop may be in for a rude awakening if their expectations do not match reality.

Another benefit is that the current employee can help the new employee get settled into the company. This will give the current employee a morale boost, because it always feels good to recruit somebody to the team and help them along in the early stages of employment. In addition, the new employee will likely feel obliged to do a good job, because they don't want to make their friend look bad by not doing well.

When considering employee referrals, you should take into account who is referring the candidate. Remember, birds of a feather flock together. If a mediocre employee recommends somebody they know, then you should be skeptical. However, a recommendation from one of your star performers should carry more weight. For the most part, good employees are not going to refer somebody they do not think will succeed in a position. They also know that the performance of the employee they vouched for will reflect on them.

Even though many employee referrals will turn out to be good candidates, you should promise your current employees that candidates they refer will be considered and nothing more. You don't want employees thinking that because they know someone who has the minimum qualifications that they will automatically get the position. You should let your employees know up front to not take it personally if you don't hire somebody they refer. Hiring somebody for a position just because you, one of your friends, or somebody else in your organization knows them is the wrong move if they are not the best person for the job.

Also, you should be careful about hiring employees from other departments within your own company. You need to be cautious about potentially burning a bridge with other managers by taking away their star employees. In addition, some unscrupulous managers might recommend a substandard employee from their department just to get rid of them. However, sometimes an employee who does not work out in another company or department may perform well for you.

Finally, if you feel uneasy about a candidate, you are usually better off not hiring them even if you have an open position that needs to be filled. It is better to take a little more time and effort to find the right employee rather than be stuck with a mediocre one. The old adage "measure twice, cut once" certainly applies. However, remember that no manager will always make the right choice when it comes to hiring employees.

Hire for Attitude, Train for Skill

In the hiring process, a general rule of thumb is to hire for attitude and train for skill. A person's attitude is so embedded and nearly impossible to change, while the skills that the employee needs to acquire can often be learned more easily. Somebody who is unfriendly, difficult to work with, and lazy will usually be a poor hire even if they have the experience and skills to do the job. It usually doesn't take long before they have a cancerous effect on the organization by bringing their negative attitude to the position and adversely affecting everybody they work with.

However, a candidate with the right attitude should be strongly considered because many skills can be learned in a short period of time. For example, if a position requires knowledge of a certain computer program, you can send the employee to a training class to acquire that skill. It would be a big mistake to eliminate an otherwise high quality candidate, because they do not have experience with a software program that can be taught in a one or two day class. The training costs are almost certainly much cheaper than the costs down the road of hiring somebody with a poor attitude.

Of course, there are limits to this maxim. Typically, the higher level the position, the less this rule applies. There is a point where the training the employee needs is too costly. And, obviously, technical knowledge is extremely important in a lot of positions (e.g. CPA, professional engineer, etc.). Therefore, you can't always just hire somebody with a good attitude if they don't have the skills needed for the position and they can't be acquired easily. But it is good general rule to keep in mind so you don't rule out a potential employee who could turn out really well with a little training.

When assessing candidates, you should be sure to differentiate between the essential requirements for a job and the preferences you have for the position. You don't want an otherwise good candidate to rule themselves out and not apply for the job because they don't exactly meet the preferred requirements. For example, sometimes experience in a certain field may be necessary. But a lot of times the employee can get up to speed on the intricacies of an industry in a brief period of time.

For example, imagine you are hiring a manager for a customer service call-in center. Here is a summary of the top two candidates from which you have to choose:

Candidate #1 - She is currently a manager of a nice restaurant and has been in that industry with three companies for a total of fifteen years. The interview went extremely well and your initial impression was confirmed when all of her previous managers spoke very highly of her. She said she has grown really tired of the restaurant industry due to all of the nights and weekends she has had to work and wants to make a permanent change to a Monday through Friday, nine to five type of work week. The only concern you have is that she does not have any experience in a customer service call-in center.

Candidate #2 - He currently manages a customer

service call-in center that is very similar to yours. He has nine years of overall experience in call-in centers with three being as a manager. Based on his experience, this candidate is certainly qualified to do the job. But you were not overly impressed with him in the interview. In addition, both of his previous managers that you were able to contact gave lukewarm reviews of him. He also seems to jump from job to job quite often.

So which one would you choose? When considering this question, think about how you define experience. Has the first candidate had experience managing a customer service call-in center? No. Has the first candidate had experience managing lower-level employees in a high stress environment? Absolutely. In reality, although the industries are different, the skills needed to manage a restaurant and the skills needed to manage a customer service call-in center are quite similar. Therefore, the first candidate seems to be a much more attractive option once you take this into consideration.

One significant benefit of hiring for attitude and training for skill is that your pool of potentially outstanding candidates greatly increases. Here is an example that shows the benefits of being open-minded to candidates who have the right attitude but don't have the particular experience you want.

Paul Kopplow is the transportation manager for an upscale Denver hotel. He manages fourteen shuttle drivers who take the hotel guests to and from the airport. The hotel shuttles are large enough to require a commercial driver's license, and a lot of hotels compete for a small pool of qualified drivers. This makes staffing a perpetual problem. At one point, Paul was short three drivers and was scrambling to fill the positions.

Since finding three qualified candidates immediately was unlikely, he cast a wider net in his search. Before accepting the position as transportation manager, Paul was a shift supervisor at one of the local plants. About a month earlier, the plant was shut down and several of his previous shift workers were out of work. There were four people that he worked with who were standout employees on his shift, so he decided to contact them to see if they still needed a job. One of the employees had just accepted a position at another plant, but the other three were thrilled to have the chance to work for Paul at the hotel.

None of the three men had ever been a driver before. But at the plant, all of them worked hard, got along well with their co-workers, and never had any unexcused absences. So Paul hired them and put them through an intensive course to get their commercial driver's license. Each of them passed with flying colors and has been a standout employee on his staff for a little over a year.

Another factor involving the attitudes of prospective employees is to consider how well a prospective candidate will fit in with current employees. After all, team chemistry is important. You want to hire people who are qualified to do the work, but they also need to be able to work harmoniously with your other employees. A candidate who seems capable of doing the work of a particular job well can still be the wrong person to hire if they have a negative effect on your other employees.

Imagine you are hiring a person for a position that will support three college professors in various administrative functions involving their research. The professors are highly regarded in their fields, but they love to kid around with each other and are always game for the occasional practical joke. Some other people in the department affectionately refer to them as "The Three Stooges."

Your first area of concern in hiring should be how well a particular candidate can do the tasks involved in the position. But a close second would be finding somebody who has the personality to fit in well with Moe, Larry, and Curly. If you have a candidate that seems to act very reserved and proper, you should probably not hire that person, because there will likely be friction between the two parties once they start working together.

Summary

The first rule of management is to surround yourself with high quality employees. The talent level of your personnel will have a major impact on how successful you are as a manager.

COMMANDMENT II

TRAIN EMPLOYEES WELL

"Because we entrust the Starbucks brand to the hands of the baristas (employees), it's vitally important that we hire great people and imbue them with our passion for coffee. We do that through a training program whose sophistication and depth are rare in retail." [4]

—Howard Schultz
Founder and former CEO, Starbucks

The training period is the last step of acquiring an employee to fill a position. You have already searched through applications, done interviews, and made an offer that was accepted. Because of all of the work that has been done, you might be tempted to slack off a little on the training of the new employee. This is especially true if you have gotten behind on some of your work because of the time you have spent finding a person for the position. However, be sure to resist these urges because these formative days, weeks, and months are a critical time. Cutting corners on training employees will only create greater difficulties down the road.

Elements of Effective Employee Training

Your goal during the training period is to teach new employees what they need to know so they can be a functioning member of the team as soon as possible. Effective training programs have numerous benefits. They can accelerate the learning process, make employee morale high from the beginning, reduce employee turnover, establish lines of communication between you and the employee, and create a bond between the employee and the company.

On the other hand, training employees ineffectively stunts the growth of new employees by making them go through unnecessary frustrations. When employees start a new job, there is a lot of nervousness, some excitement, and even a little fear. Employees want to blend in to their environment and be accepted as soon as possible. If the initial starting period is too uncomfortable for employees, they may start to wonder if they made the right decision to take the job and may leave soon after they are hired.

A successful training program should include information about the overall company as well as the employee's department and individual job. This can include discussing the policies and procedures of the company, key executives, culture, etc. You should also give a full description of what products and services the company provides as well as information about its customers and competitors. In addition, the employee should be taken around to other departments in the company and given the names and titles of people that will be important to them as well as tips regarding their work styles and personalities. Above all, however, you should communicate to the employee through your actions that they are valued and you will make sure that they are given every opportunity to succeed.

Once the new employee has been informed about the company, you can begin training them in their job. Unless your company provides the training your employees will need, you should have control over as much of the job training in your department as possible. This is not something you should delegate unless one of your employees is the only one with expertise in that particular area. The reason is that whoever does the training sets the standard and has the implied authority. And you need to be the one who sets the standards for your employees and has the authority over them. Employees who are trained in their jobs by someone else will likely go to that person when they have questions in the future and you should want them coming to you.

Once the specific job training starts, remember that the quickest way for employees to learn a new skill is for them to jump in and do it. You can only go so far by explaining something to the employee. After you go through the process of explaining a task to an employee once, let the employee get their feet wet while you sit back and give guidance when they need it. You should also encourage the new employee to ask as many questions as possible and do your best to give thorough answers. Although a lot of questions they ask will be very basic and the number of questions may test your patience, try to put yourself in their shoes and remember what it is like to start in a new position.

During the training process, you should allow employees to make mistakes and then use them to teach employees where they went wrong. Employees are much better off making mistakes in front of you rather than on their own after the initial training period. You should also ask them questions and have them explain to you what they have been taught to make sure they truly understand what they are doing. In the initial stages of training, you should not just accept it when employees say they understand what you taught them. Let them show you they understand. In addition, be sure to give employees a sense of how what they are doing fits into the big picture. It is easy to focus only on the steps necessary to do a task, but giving employees a broader view will instill a much deeper understanding of how their role relates to the whole operation.

Managers should give a lot of assurance during the employee's training period. It is very important to praise employees when they do a task correctly. If a task is done partially correct, then praise what was done right and tactfully let the employee know where a mistake was made and how it should be corrected. The training period is usually a very uncomfortable time for new employees. They need to know that they are making progress and you will be there to help them when they need it. During this time, don't expect an employee to be perfect, just expect them to improve. You want to do what you can to build the employee's confidence. If employees have some early success in their job, they will feel like they are a contributing member of the team and will likely have a favorable first impression of the company.

Finally, the training period should be viewed as a process and not a one time event. A lot of questions that employees will have can be answered in the first few days and it won't be very long before the number of questions tapers off sharply. However, you should not think that this will be the end of the assistance you will need to give them. Every once in a while, they will need to come to you to get a question answered and it is critical that you make yourself available to them. This will allow employees to complete what they are doing and know exactly what to do when the situation arises in the future.

Examples

Here are two examples that show the consequences of improperly and properly training employees:

Kevin Sullivan was hired as a salesman by a medical equipment company in Baltimore. His experience selling to hospitals in his previous jobs helped him land the position. Kevin was excited about the job, but knew that he needed to get some training on the products that his new company offered. Even though he was still selling to hospitals, the product line was much different than what he had sold before.

However, when he arrived at his new job, he was shocked to find out that his new company didn't plan on giving him any training on the products he would be selling. Basically, he was given the keys to a company car and told to get the job done without any knowledge of the products. Although Kevin was a good salesman, he was in way over his head. He felt like a person who couldn't swim and the swimming instructor just pushed him into the pool and told him to figure out how to swim on his own.

Therefore, when he would meet with a potential client at a hospital, he could not even answer some of the basic questions that they would have. The customers would get very frustrated, because they felt their time was being wasted. After desperately trying to teach himself what he needed to know about the products he was selling, Kevin finally got so frustrated that he quit just a month after he started.

Starbucks is a company that does an outstanding job training their employees. They give each new hire, including part-time employees, twenty four hours of training which is remarkable for their industry. The training is done by either store managers or district managers and includes basic employee orientation as well as other various courses.[5] New employees watch a video where the CEO tells them about the company's history, his experience there, and how happy he is to have them join Starbucks. They also participate in mock customer service scenarios. The result: Employee turnover at Starbucks is usually around 60% which is much lower than the industry average of 150%.[6]

Summary

The training period is the bridge between the time employees walk through the door their first day until they are comfortable doing the job on their own. A thorough training program will give each new employee a much better chance to succeed in their job.

COMMANDMENT III

TELL EMPLOYEES WHAT YOU EXPECT OF THEM, THEN DON'T MICROMANAGE

"Be like jockey Willie Shoemaker. He's the best in the business because he has the lightest touch on the reins. They say the horse never knows he's there --unless he's needed." [7]

—Harvey Mackay
Founder and CEO, Mackay Envelope

Most managers possess the trait of wanting to be in control. They have the self-confidence to be in charge and succeed or fail according to the decisions they make. This deserves admiration. Unfortunately, some managers overstep their bounds and try to control too much. The result is the dreaded micro-manager.

Micromanagers give employees tasks to do and then meddle by analyzing every minute detail involved in the job. They second guess decisions, discourage individual problem solving, and throw trust out the window. When employees are micromanaged, they feel disrespected and insignificant, because the manager's actions make it seem as though they have no confidence in the employee's ability. Before you know it, employee morale takes a nose dive.

Why Micromanaging Occurs

Some managers have trouble delegating because they feel they are losing decision making power. The more employees are empowered, the less the manager feels needed. However, managers should realize that their job is not to do all of the work. They should not be solving their employees' problems for them. On the contrary, the manager's job is to get things done *through people* by giving them guidance, encouragement, and a sense of ownership in their jobs.

First-time managers often have a tendency to micromanage. Employees who are promoted to a management position are usually ones who have excelled at their jobs. They are used to having total control over their work and have difficulty letting go, because they have never trusted anybody else with it before. They probably got ahead by continually taking on more responsibility and paying close attention to detail. As a manager, though, this can get them into serious trouble. Continually taking on more responsibility can turn into doing employees' work for them. And paying close attention to detail can turn into micromanaging. Even though letting go after being in control is difficult, new managers have to unlearn these behaviors to be effective.

Some managers resist giving employees the freedom to make their own decisions, because they have a very difficult time trusting employees. Even though every once in a while an employee will abuse your trust, you can't let that ruin the trust you have with all of your other workers. Employees will usually delight you when you trust them to figure out their own way to do a job. Trust is like a self-fulfilling prophecy. When you trust workers, you are communicating the message "I believe in you." Most of the time, your employees will thank you by fulfilling your expectations to the best of their ability.

However, even employees with good intentions will still make honest mistakes every once in a while despite trying to do their best. These mistakes should be treated as learning opportunities. But what should be done if employees are given the freedom to do their jobs and they are still constantly doing things wrong? When this happens, you need to find somebody who can actually do that job. The goal should be to hire good employees so you don't have to always worry about them.

Let Employees Know Exactly What You Want

If you should not meddle, then what is the right approach to take? First, you need to set crystal clear objectives for employees. If employees don't understand what is expected of them, then they will never know how well they are doing. And you can't assume that employees know what you want unless you tell them. Therefore, it is critical to thoroughly communicate your expectations when an employee is first hired. Then, your expectations should be conveyed every time you give an employee a task to do or when job responsibilities change. When employees know what is expected of them, they don't sit around and wait for their manager to tell them what to do. This also allows employees to gauge how they are performing, because they can compare what they have accomplished with what is expected of them.

When a manager instructs an employee to do a task, they should keep in mind that the way an instruction is given can have a tremendous impact on how well it is done. Employees will react very differently to instructions depending on whether they are perceived as respectful or disrespectful. Therefore, when managers issue instructions, they should ask "Could you please do this?" rather than giving a direct order such as "You must do this." The manager should then follow up by saying "Thank you" or "I appreciate it." This tactful approach subtly makes employees feel important, needed, and respected.

When employees are ordered around, they feel patronized and belittled. By issuing instructions in a polite manner, you are showing them respect. Employees will then show their appreciation by taking a more positive approach to the task. This will, in turn, result in them being more productive. The difference in how an instruction is worded is so small, but the reaction from employees will be much different depending on which approach is taken.

However, you should realize that not bossing employees around does not mean that you become a pushover. When you ask employees to do tasks in a polite manner, they will usually respond positively to this gesture of respect. In some cases, however, employees will interpret this politeness as a sign of weakness and ignore the instruction. When this occurs, you should reissue the instruction in an increasingly firm manner. Most employees will straighten out once you use this approach with them.

Give Employees the Freedom to Make Decisions

Once employees understand exactly what you want and when you want it, you need to give them the freedom to figure out how the task should be completed. In general, you should not worry about how an employee solves a problem as long as the problem is solved. The result is more important than the process. Also, when you give employees the freedom to get the end result you desire, you are putting the responsibility on them. If you were to tell them exactly how to do their work, you could be blamed if things did not go right.

However, empowering employees does not mean that they can do anything they want. You should articulate how much leeway employees have when making decisions. There will be certain activities that employees can't do their own way, and you should make sure that you communicate that to them in those instances.

When giving an employee an instruction, you can offer suggestions to help make the job easier before they begin the assignment. Especially with longer assignments, you should get some feedback from employees about how they plan to approach the project. If the employee is headed down the wrong path or could complete the work in a more efficient manner, you can propose other alternatives that might make the assignment go a little smoother.

In addition, you should monitor an employee's progress so they don't get sidetracked. This can be done by mutually deciding on times that you will follow up with them to make sure the project is going as planned. This will allow you to answer any questions the employee may have and correct any errors the employee may be making.

To illustrate the extent to which you should be involved once a task is assigned, imagine you assign an employee the task of driving from Los Angeles to New York and allow him a week in which to do it. A micromanager would decide exactly what route he should take, exactly how many hours he should drive per day, and exactly where he should eat and sleep. The micromanager would then follow him all across the country to make sure that he carried out the instructions properly. That seems like a slight waste of time, doesn't it? Does it really matter if the employee goes through Denver, Chicago, and Cleveland instead of Phoenix, Dallas, and Washington D.C. as long as he arrives in New York safely and on time?

Instead, the situation should be handled by letting the employee decide how he is going to complete the task in the allotted time frame. You should first tell the employee exactly what you want. You must be sure that you are not giving vague instructions. For example, you don't just want to say "I need you to drive from the West Coast to the East Coast." The employee needs to know where to start, where to finish, and when it needs to be done. You can then offer advice up front that will make the trip easier such as notifying him of places where there might be heavy road construction or adverse weather conditions.

Once the trip begins, you should ask the employee to call every few days to assure you that the trip is going as planned. Since the employee knows what is expected of him, he can check his progress any time he wants without having to ask you for feedback. However, if any problems or questions arise, the employee should be able to contact you and together you both can figure out the proper action to take.

The point of this example is that many roads can get you to your intended destination. But getting there, not how you get there, is what is most important.

In addition, managers should not confuse activity with progress. There are some employees who can stay quite busy and yet get little work of substance done. On the other hand, some employees are marvelously efficient. Granted, working hard will usually help to get results, but only if the employee is also working smart. For example, consider the employee who is supposed to drive from Los Angeles to New York. Imagine you call him a few days into the trip to check on his progress. He says, "Things are going great. All of my non-sleeping hours have been spent driving. I'm really busting my tail." Then, you ask "Where are you?" The employee responds, "Seattle." The employee drove through Las Vegas, Salt Lake City, and Portland to get there. Obviously, this is not the optimal way to get to New York. The most important question isn't "How many hours have you driven?", but "How far away are you from New York?" The results are what matter, not necessarily constant activity.

Under normal circumstances, employees can be given the freedom to make their own decisions and everybody is happy. However, as crazy as it may sound, some employees actually want to be micromanaged. These types of employees keep asking questions without making any attempt to make a decision themselves. They constantly bring problems to the manager instead of solutions. Although these employees might have a difficult time adjusting when the bulk of the responsibility is placed on them, they need to be strongly encouraged to make decisions on their own. You don't want employees delegating back up to you.

However, every once in a while, managers should consider stepping in and helping employees with their workload. For example, a manager could help out when an employee gets swamped with work due to unlucky circumstances beyond their control. When this happens, you don't want to say, "Hey, it's your problem." Even helping the employee a little will go a long way in these instances.

Finally, managers must understand that the rule against micromanaging only applies to fully trained employees. During the initial phase of employment, managers *should* spend a lot of time with employees to make sure that they feel sufficiently comfortable with what they are supposed to do. Any time you are training a new employee, there is going to be an adjustment period when you have to communicate more and keep a closer eye on them. The key is to gradually step back and let them do their work once they have learned how to do the job.

Example

Here is an example of a company that gives their employees an overall objective along with the freedom to accomplish that goal:

Nordstrom, the fashion retailer who is legendary for their customer service, gives employees virtually total freedom to make customers happy. For example, salespeople are allowed to take back any returned merchandise even if it has been damaged by the customer[8], match the price of a competitor without consulting their manager[9], and sell products from any department in the store, not just their own.[10]

The Nordstrom employee handbook is on a 5" x 8" card and reads as follows:

Welcome to Nordstrom

We're glad to have you with our company. Our number one goal is to provide outstanding customer serv-

ice. Set both your personal and professional goals high. We have great confidence in your ability to achieve them. So our employee handbook is very simple.

We have only one rule...

Our only rule:

Use good judgment in all situations.

Please feel free to ask your Department Manager, Store Manager or Human Resource office any question any time.[11]

Summary

Don't be a micromanager. Let employees know what needs to be done and then get out of their way.

COMMANDMENT IV

LEAD BY EXAMPLE

"No psychological weapon is more potent than example. An executive who seeks to achieve results through the people who work under his direction must himself demonstrate at least as high a standard of performance as he hopes to get from his subordinates...When an executive's bad example or his double standards become known, morale and output plummet in his department." [12]

—J. Paul Getty
Founder and former President, Getty Oil

The most effective way to teach employees how to act is through your own example. Whenever you do something, the message communicated to employees is "This is acceptable behavior."

Employee See, Employee Do

As a manager, think about all of the characteristics your perfect employee would have. For example, they would: work hard; work smart; treat customers well; show up on time every day; challenge the status quo and think of better ways to do things; work well with others; pay attention to details; dress appropriately; promptly return messages; work late if necessary; finish tasks early; do things right the first time; hold themselves accountable for their mistakes; be enjoyable to work with; have a standard of excellence; have a pleasant demeanor; be loyal; be thrifty with the company money; adhere to company policy; not miss work due to unexcused absences, and practice the company's values.

Now, apply that standard to yourself and think about how well you live up to it.

Do you work hard? Do you work smart? Do you treat customers well? Do you show up on time every day? Do you challenge the status quo and think of better ways to do things? Do you work well with others? Do you pay attention to details? Do you dress appropriately? Do you promptly return messages? Do you work late if necessary? Do you finish tasks early? Do you do things right the first time? Do you hold yourself accountable for your mistakes? Are you enjoyable to work with? Do you have a standard of excellence? Do you have a pleasant demeanor? Are you loyal? Are you thrifty with the company money? Do you adhere to company policy? Do you not miss work due to unexcused absences? Do you practice the company's values?

You should never ask anybody to do anything that you are not willing to do yourself. If you do, then you are facing an uphill battle. The line "Do as I say, not as I do" should not be used by managers. You not only have to talk the talk, but you have to walk the walk. However, if you set a good example, then you will raise the bar for employees. If you act the right way, you can always trump employees who don't comply with the subtle unspoken expectation "I do it, so you should be able to do it, too."

Examples

Here are five examples that discuss the concept of leading by example:

A large Midwestern media company faced declining profits in a recession and was forced to cut their expenses. Instead of having a large number of layoffs, the top management decided to freeze everybody's salary for a year. They also cut the salaries of the high-level managers by five percent. Even though it was tough not getting their raises, the employees understood that they had to sacrifice for the good of the company. And to have the high-level managers go beyond just getting their salaries frozen by taking a five percent cut showed that they were sacrificing along with them.

I used to live in a suburb of Denver, Colorado. The post office that was closest to my house was usually very busy. You pretty much expected to wait in line for five or ten minutes whenever you went there. Most of the time, the customers were pretty patient. However, every once in a while somebody would get very upset.

On three different occasions, I saw another customer have an "I want to speak to the manager" moment. The employee working the counter would reluctantly say "OK, hold on a second" and then go back to get the manager. Then, the employee would come back about a minute or two later and say "Sorry, the manager can't come up to the front right now." The customers, who were determined to speak their mind to the manager, would say "That's fine. I'll wait until the manager is available." The employee would respond by saying "The manager isn't going to be available any time soon." After it was clear the manager was never going to come to the counter, the customers would give up and storm out of the post office.

It is obvious that the manager just didn't want to deal with any customers who had a problem with the post office. That behavior set a terrible example for employees. The message sent to employees was: If you don't feel like dealing with customers that have a problem with the post office, then you should just ignore them until they go away. The manager's example set a very low standard for employees to follow.

Patricia Simmons has been the general manager for an upscale Seattle restaurant for the past eight years. During her time there, she has only missed work on three occasions. And each time was when she was either in the emergency room or attending to a close family member there. When employees don't show up to work in the restaurant business, it puts a tremendous burden on the rest of the staff because somebody has to do that job. Patricia fully understands this and knows that she has to set the standard for all of her employees. There have been many times when she could have stayed home, but instead she toughed it out and came to work. Because her employees know that she will always be there for them, they do their best to make it to work every time they are supposed to be there.

Many years ago one of my best friends and I took a trip to New York City. During the week we were there, we made a one day side trip to Boston to visit his brother and see a mutual friend of ours. We spent the day sightseeing and got to his brother's house in the evening. Neither of us had eaten much all day so we ventured out to get a meal and decided on a take out sandwich café that was nearby.

As we walked in, I noticed two employees just hanging out by the register talking to each other. It was forty five minutes until closing and nobody was there so they were just killing time until they could close. After I ordered, I was looking around as they made our sandwiches and noticed a piece of paper on the wall right next to the register that had the heading "If you have nothing to do, read this list." Below the heading were thirty or forty activities for employees to do such as "Sweep the floor", "Take out the garbage", "Clean the bathroom", "Wipe down the counters", etc. Then, there was a signature on the bottom of the piece of paper with the title "District Manager" below it.

I asked one of the employees what that was all about.

He said that a couple of months before then the district manager stopped by unexpectedly one night and saw a couple of employees doing nothing since there weren't any customers there. After witnessing that, the district manager immediately went back to the office, wrote up the list, and posted it by the register. I asked the employee what all of the employees thought about the list and he said "What do you think? We hate it."

As a customer, the message I got was "Your sandwich is being made by a lazy person." That is not a message you want to communicate to customers. And from an employee's perspective, the embarrassment not only of having the sign up, but having the sign up where customers could see it, killed morale and motivation. After all, they were still doing nothing when we walked in so it was obvious their behavior didn't change. Clearly, this approach was not the correct one to take to fix the problem.

The ultimate question is: How should that situation have been handled? In this instance, starting with a softer approach would have probably been better. The district manager should have politely greeted the employees, put his items back in the office, and then picked up a broom and started sweeping. Then, he could have said "Hey guys, could I get one of you to wipe down the counters and the other to take out the garbage? I appreciate it." By doing this, the district manager would have communicated to the employees what to do through his own example.

Then, the district manager should have had a private conversation with the store manager the next time they met to discuss what happened. He could ask the store manager if this happens a lot. If it does, the store manager should be told in a tactful manner that the assistant managers and employees should be informed of other duties that can be done when it is not busy.

The movie *Saving Private Ryan* is about a group of soldiers in World War II who are on a mission to save one soldier after his brothers have been killed in combat. There is a moral argument about whether or not it is fair to put the lives of several soldiers at risk just to make an attempt to save one soldier. The soldiers on the mission are led by Capt. John Miller (played by Tom Hanks) and they clearly communicate that they don't feel it is the right thing to do.

As they are searching for Private Ryan, the soldiers in the group discuss their feelings and ask Capt. Miller what he thinks. Even though it is pretty obvious that he feels the same way as they do, he tells them that he thinks it is a worthy mission. This is a classic case of leading by example. He could have compromised the mission and destroyed morale by sharing his true feelings, but he chose to be faithful to his orders even though he disagreed with them.

There may come a time when your employees disagree with you, but you don't want them undermining your authority by not going along with your decision. By giving your all even when you disagree with a decision given to you from above, you are teaching your employees how to act when they disagree with you.

Summary

Whether what you do is good, bad, or indifferent, your actions set the stage for how your employees behave.

COMMANDMENT V

PRAISE GOOD WORK

"Nothing else can quite substitute for a few well-chosen, well-timed, sincere words of praise. They're absolutely free--and worth a fortune." [13]

—Sam Walton
Founder and former CEO, Wal-Mart

Managers should not underestimate the power that praise has on employee morale. When employees are complimented, they get a warm, fuzzy, magical feeling inside. In addition, the manager's job becomes easier because positive reinforcement of actions gets those actions repeated. Employees will begin to seek out more ways to earn praise by working harder and more productively.

Why Praise Matters

To illustrate how important it is for people to receive recognition, think about all of the keepsakes of success that we retain to remind ourselves of the good feeling of praise. For example, a good friend of mine, Dean, died a few years ago from cancer. A few months later, Dean's

Dad invited me to come to his house to select something to remember him by. In his closet, Dean had fifteen or twenty trophies that he had earned throughout his life. Several of them seemed to be quite old so I looked at all of the dates. The oldest one was from 1970. He had kept that trophy for thirty years, because it made him feel like a winner.

Some employees don't go above and beyond the call of duty even when they know it will help the company, because they think nobody will recognize their efforts. Their attitude is, "Even if I do this, nobody is going to notice anyway. So what's the point?" Even though your workload is likely heavy, do your best to stay informed about all of the good things that your employees are doing and look for opportunities to praise them. You don't want to just give feedback to employees when they do something wrong. That is an easy trap to fall into.

Here is an example of an employee who thought he wasn't doing a good job because he was never praised:

Ken Robbins is a mechanical engineer for an engineering firm in Houston. His best friend at work is one of the top civil engineers in the company. Ken went out to lunch one day with a civil engineer who reported directly to his best friend. Ken's friend had always raved to him about how good this employee was. But during lunch, the employee confided in Ken that he was really worried that his manager wasn't happy with his performance. Ken burst out, "Are you kidding me? He talks my ear off bragging about you." The employee was thrilled to hear that, but surprised because he had never been told that he had been doing a good job.

Later that day, Ken went back and told his friend about this. His friend said, "I'm not sure why he would think I wasn't happy with his performance. After all, I have never gotten on him for anything since he has been here." Ken replied, "Yeah, but you never told him he was doing a good job either. Whether it's right or wrong, it sounds like he didn't get any feedback and just assumed the worst. But you should have never given him the chance to make that assumption."

How to Praise

Most managers are in a position where they have very little time and no money to commit to a formal recognition program. But you don't even have to go that far to be effective. You can still praise employees in many different simple ways even if you are really busy and have no money to distribute. This can include: giving them a phone call; sending an e-mail with a carbon copy to a high-level manager; telling them face to face; writing them a note and putting it on their computer; sneaking a letter in with their paycheck; leaving them a voice mail, or passing along a customer satisfaction card that compliments the employee. Also, you can let employees know if another manager or employee says something nice about their work. These people will probably not feel as comfortable saying that directly to the employee. But you can brighten their day if you discreetly pass along the kind words to them.

Managers should realize that the praise is the gift and a certificate or plaque is only the wrapping. The gift is what is important. A note telling an employee that they did a good job only takes a few minutes to write, but the positive impact is still the same. Plus, it can have a lasting effect because employees will be able to look at the note or printed e-mail whenever they want. In addition, with an e-mail they can forward it to their close friends and family and say "Hey, look what my boss sent me!" Praise can be priceless and it doesn't have to cost a penny.

In addition, praise will have more of an impact if you apply it to a specific action and give it close to when the behavior took place. You want to let employees know exactly what they did right as soon as possible. Then, employees will connect the praise with the specific work they have done well. This will reinforce the behavior which will increase the chances that it will be repeated in the future.

Consider the feedback options you have if one of your employees turns in a monthly report two days early and makes some design improvements to it:

Option #1 - Say nothing.

Option #2 - Say thank you to the employee three days later.

Option #3 - Thank the employee two days later for turning the report in before the deadline and making the design improvements.

Option #4 - Thank the employee that day for turning in the report two days early and coming up with two new color pie charts that were included on page two and page four.

At a minimum, you should have gone with option #2. But option #4 is the best, because the praise given is the most specific and closest to when the action took place.

Also, although it is good to praise your employees, managers should not overdo it. If you do, the value of the praise will be diminished and your employees will probably feel that you are trying to manipulate them. On the other hand, never praising employees is not the best way to go either. The answer lies somewhere in the middle of these two extremes depending on the individual employee.

In addition, all praise given to employees should be genuine. Praising employees halfheartedly or insincerely when it is not deserved can do more damage than giving no praise at all. If you praise an employee who does not deserve it, then you are just encouraging mediocre behavior to continue. Also, it is a good idea to utilize different methods of praise so it does not become mechanical.

Consider this analogy when analyzing the relationship between praising employees and employee morale and motivation. Imagine you have a plant and you don't ever feed it. How long do you think the plant will live? Obviously, not very long. The leaves will soon become brown and wilted. What about if you put the right amount of water on the plant? Then, you will give the plant the best chance to be healthy and live as long as possible. The leaves will be green, firm, and vibrant. What if you feed the plant too much water? This will hurt the plant, because it only needs so much water to be healthy. The point is that the plant is the morale and motivation of your employees and the water is praise.

Recognize All Deserving Employees

Many reward systems are predicated on celebrating the feats of the elite performers. No matter how deserving the recipient of the award is, however, the other employees will likely feel slighted because they are not being praised for their efforts. Because people tend to compare themselves to one another, when another employee is recognized and they are not, it is natural for employees to wonder what is wrong with them.

There is a commercial that recently came out that has two employees who work at a retail business that looks like Wal-Mart or Target. They are talking to each other in amazement about the star employee who hasn't ever called in sick to work for several years. At the end of the commercial, the star employee is named the employee of the month for the tenth straight month and she celebrates to the chagrin of the other two employees. Even though this was only supposed to be funny, there is a lot of truth in it.

With praise, your goal should not be to only recognize the top performer. Your goal should be to improve overall productivity. And the productivity of your organization is not based on one person doing well, so it doesn't make sense to only praise the top employee. With any group of employees, some are going to be better than others. But it is extremely important to give praise to any employee when it is deserved. Therefore, instead of only singling out the top performers, managers should also recognize the efforts of the other employees.

In a similar fashion, one of the traps some managers fall into when it comes to praising employees is the Superman syndrome. Superman can foil Lex Luther's evil plans, leap tall buildings in a single bound, run as fast as high speed trains, and still have time for Lois Lane. Many managers are fortunate to have a Superman or Superwoman working for them. These dynamite employees are deservedly lavished with praise. But the reality is that not every employee is capable of being a Superman or Superwoman. Some of your employees will show up consistently every day and quietly get their work done with minimal help just as they are expected. They are not going to "Wow" you, but they also never give you any problems. These employees are often easily overlooked, but they need praise, too. You should remind yourself to show appreciation for what they do, because their importance will become really obvious if they are ever not there. This doesn't mean that you should reward mediocrity. It just means to try to show appreciation for the everyday things that employees are doing well.

Celebrate Employee Birthdays

Although this is unrelated to work performance, another way managers can recognize employees is by celebrating their birthdays. All you have to do is get a card for them that everybody else can sign. This will show that you care about the employee as a person, because their birthday is probably the most important day of the year for them. In fact, how much a company celebrates birthdays is an unusual but fairly accurate indicator of how much everybody cares about each other. It is pretty sad that you can spend just as much time with a group of people at work as you do with your own family, but not celebrate each other's birthdays. That makes the business a cold place to work. However, if an employee doesn't want their birthday celebrated, then you should honor their wishes. The best time to find out if celebrating their birthday is a problem is by asking them when they are first hired.

Summary

Mark Twain once said "I can live for two months on a good compliment." Praise is an extremely powerful motivator because it is nourishment for people's self-esteem, gives them a sense of importance, and fulfills their intense hunger for recognition.

COMMANDMENT VI

SHARE INFORMATION

"Almost anyone at Dell can explain the fundamental concepts that our business is based on. That's because we spend a tremendous amount of time communicating what's going on, what we're planning to do, and what everyone needs to do to help us achieve our goals." [14]

—Michael Dell
Founder and CEO, Dell Computer

Have you ever tried to walk through your house when it is completely dark? You have a vague idea of what is around you, but you still have to walk slowly and reach your arms out to make sure nothing is right in front of you. Despite your precautions, you will often stub your toe or bump your shoulder on a wall or piece of furniture. Then, when you reach your intended destination and turn the light on, the path you should have taken is perfectly clear.

An employee who lacks information is in the same position as a person walking through their house when it is completely dark. They are unable to move quickly and act decisively, because they don't have enough information to make sure they are going down the right path.

Keep Employees in the Loop

Information is the tool that allows employees to do better work by increasing their understanding of their situation. The more information employees have, the better they are able to do their jobs. Employees who are not given enough information feel like they are operating with one arm tied behind their back. They are unable to make certain decisions, because they don't want to make assumptions that may create more problems than they solve. Some managers complain that their employees can't see the big picture. But how are they supposed to see the big picture if they are not given the information to understand what is going on?

When you share information with employees, the message being sent is that you think highly of them which builds trust and gives employee morale and motivation a boost. In addition, when employees know what is going on, they are much more likely to understand the issues that you face in your position. It allows them to see where they can make a difference. On the other hand, employees will never have the ability or desire to help you if you hoard information from them.

For example, imagine you are the manager of a restaurant and one of your job performance measures is the feedback given on customer comment cards. Instead of keeping this information to yourself, you should share it with employees. You could do this by having monthly meetings to discuss the positive or negative comments. Employees could then discuss ways to improve which would make them more likely to feel responsible for the results.

The next time you acquire important pieces of information you should be thinking "Who also needs to know this?" If you don't, you are holding your employees back. For example, if you go to a meeting with other managers, you should seriously consider gathering your employees or sending out an e-mail to give them a summary of what was discussed and how it affects the department. Employees will appreciate it when you do this.

Managers should also share information with employees about company strategy, sales, expenses, competitors, etc. The employees you manage should know why the company or department exists, the role of each employee, who the main customers are, and what the guidelines are for being successful. They also need to know about the other departments in the company, why they exist, and what they are trying to achieve. In addition, any change in policy should be discussed with the employees who are impacted by it.

Hoarding Information

There are some managers that hoard information from their employees. They absorb information from their managers and peers, but they make a conscious decision not to pass it along to their employees. Inside information is a source of power and status. Why share it when you can have it all to yourself?

Managers who hoard information are doing a disservice to themselves and their employees. These types of managers increase their workload as a result of doing this. Their employees don't have the information to make a lot of decisions by themselves so they constantly have to check with the manager. This wastes both the manager's and the employee's time.

In addition, hoarding information breeds mistrust and miscommunication. If you don't share information, employees may get the wrong information through the grapevine. The grapevine will typically exaggerate information and put a negative spin on it. Employees will usually assume the worst when they are not informed about what is going on. For example, a company may be planning some minor layoffs over the next couple of months. But a rumor starts making its way around the company that there are going to be massive layoffs. As a result, morale plummets and lots of employees start looking for jobs and some good ones end up leaving to work elsewhere.

The root cause of hoarding information is the manager's fear of becoming unimportant. They feel their position won't be challenged by anybody if nobody else knows what they know. If employees were to have too much information, this would be perceived as a threat to the manager's status and authority. Hoarding information is a method of self-protection so other employees won't look better than they do.

Managers who hoard information will make various

excuses as to why they don't share it. Most include the assumption of employee ignorance. These include: they aren't intelligent enough to understand it, they won't know what to do with it, they aren't interested in it, they might share it with competitors, etc. All of these assumptions are usually false. You would be better served by assuming the exact opposite. But if you believe those assumptions to be true and your behavior reflects this belief, then your employees will never come close to reaching their full potential.

It may seem that you are more powerful when you keep information from your employees. But that is an illusion. Real power comes when you share information which results in an increased level of productivity and much greater loyalty from your employees. Managers who hoard information rarely move up the ladder, because teams can only be so effective when one person monopolizes the information. Ironically, managers who hoard information will be more likely to have underperforming departments which will ultimately threaten their jobs.

In a lot of companies, managers work on the second floor and regular employees work on the first floor. The information on the second floor is freely distributed to everybody else on the floor. But when an employee from the first floor asks for it, the response is "Sorry, that information is only for people that work on the second floor and it does not apply to you." The problem is that when the company profits are low and the managers stress to employees that they need to think of ways to make the company money, the employees are likely to say "That is a second floor issue and it does not apply to me."

In reality, the second floor is obviously not a floor in a building. But it does exist in management meetings, e-mails between managers, confidential memos, private conversations between managers, etc. In a corporate setting, it is the "Over $60,000 a year" club. In a fast food restaurant, it is the "Above minimum wage" club. In a factory, it is the "Anybody who supervises somebody who gets their hands dirty" club. In most businesses, there is a clear division between who has access to "high-level" information and who doesn't.

In order to maximize employee productivity and business efficiency, this line needs to be eliminated. This is not to say that all employees are equally valuable. There is a reason why people make different salaries. But just because somebody is higher on the organizational chart does not mean that they are the only one who should have access to important information.

Finally, although managers are wise to share a lot of information with employees, not every bit of company information should be distributed. Coca-Cola would be unwise to share the formula for Coke with every one of its employees. In addition, you should keep employees' salaries and personnel files confidential. And private conversations should remain private. You should not share a piece of information that your boss, a co-worker, or one of your employees has asked you to keep to yourself. In these instances, you should be honest with employees by telling them that you can't reveal that information.

Examples

Here are four examples regarding sharing information:

One of the best examples of a company that has benefited from sharing information is the Springfield Remanufacturing Corporation (SRC). In 1983, a group of managers went into deep debt and bought a struggling factory owned by International Harvester where they worked in Springfield, Missouri. On the verge of bankruptcy and with 119 jobs hanging in the balance[15], the company, led by CEO Jack Stack, opened their books to all employees, explained how the company made money, and showed employees what they could do about it.[16] Employees would meet at a specified time every week to go over the financial numbers for that period[17] which would keep everybody up to date regarding what was going on and prompt discussion of strategies for improvement.[18] The result was that from 1983 to 1991 the value of SRC's stock skyrocketed from $0.10 per share to $18.30 per share.[19]

Imagine a customer comes up to a clerk in the men's clothing department of a retail department store and inquires about the availability of a popular, expensive jacket with a high mark up. The clerk looks where the jacket is sold and says "Sorry, it looks like we are all out." Then, the customer says "Do you know when you will have any in stock?" The employee responds by saying "No, I sure don't", because he doesn't have a username and password to access the inventory management system. That customer will probably be disappointed and go to another competing department store to buy the jacket.

But what if that clerk had been given a username and password and could access that information even when his manager was not around? Then, he would have known when the next shipment of those particular jackets would be arriving at the store. Let's rewind what happened and think about how the conversation might have gone. The customer says "Do you know when you will have any in stock?" The employee responds by saying "I'm not sure, but walk over to the counter with me and I can check on the computer."

After looking up that information, the employee says "Actually, sir, we are expecting to get the next order of those jackets two days from now. If you give me the size you are looking for and your phone number, I can put one aside when the shipment arrives and call you to let you know it is here. How does that sound?" The customer replies, "That would be great, thanks."

A commercial real estate company was looking to cut expenses and decided that they had to control the amount of money they were spending on shipping packages. The concern was justified because many employees got in the habit of sending all of their packages through the overnight or two day service of the most expensive shipper who did not give them a volume discount. This added up to a significant amount of money over time. As a result, the administration and finance directors decided to only allow employees to send packages through a low cost shipper who would give them a volume discount.

After their decision was made, they sent out an e-mail to everybody in the company notifying them of the change. Within thirty minutes, several employees responded to the e-mail to complain about the new policy. A couple of them argued that they needed to use the more expensive shipper occasionally, because they had to send items that had to arrive on time such as payroll checks to the other offices or product information brochures to interested customers. The low cost shipper had the reputation of occasionally being late or losing a shipment and that was not acceptable.

The employees were most disappointed because they were not notified that there was a serious problem with the money spent shipping packages. Nobody had asked them how the problem could be solved while still meeting their respective shipping needs. Therefore, the administration and finance directors decided to postpone the implementation of the new policy to see if the employees could come up with a solution that would accomplish all of their objectives.

The employees ended up contacting one of the other high quality shippers to see if the company could get a volume discount if they let the shipper deliver all of their packages. The shipper offered a fair discount which the company eventually accepted. In addition, only the packages that absolutely had to be there in the next day or two were sent through the overnight or two day service. All of the other packages were sent through the ground service which took a few days longer but was much cheaper.

The employees also encouraged each other not to wait until the last minute to ship items. In the past, a lot of employees would wait to ship a package until a day or two before it needed to be there. The reason was they knew it would still arrive on time and they were not concerned with the cost.

The employees ended up embracing the new policy much more because they were a part of the decision making process. If the new policy would have been imposed on them without any input, it is almost certain that the employees would not have tried as hard to ship their own packages early and encouraged others to do so. In addition, they actually did a lot of the work for the managers after they postponed their initial decision by contacting the other high quality shipper and negotiating a volume discount. In hindsight, the managers should have shared the information regarding the high shipping costs with the employees from the beginning and then asked them for suggestions regarding how the problem might be solved.

A Chicago interior design company bought out a smaller competitor that had an office in the suburbs forty five minutes away. About two-thirds of the staff from the company that was bought out were laid off. The others were moved into the main Chicago office. Once the office in the suburbs was just about to be completely vacated, the office manager from the Chicago office had the calls to the office in the suburbs forwarded to the main office. But the office manager failed to tell anybody at the Chicago office that he had done that.

As a result, the main office was getting what they thought were some very strange calls for a couple of days when the office manager was away closing down the other office. Numerous times the support staff answering the phones had to say "Sorry, but you have the wrong number." The callers would often call right back since they were certain they had the right phone number. This would further agitate the people answering the phone. And the people calling, including some important customers, had no idea why the phone number they had used for so long wasn't working.

Finally, the office manager was made aware of the strange calls when he called into the main office to check up on things. He confessed that the line from the company that was bought out had been forwarded beginning two days prior to that. Needless to say, the members of the support staff at the main office were very upset. All the office manager had to do was send out a mass e-mail to everybody at the main office and none of the problems would have occurred.

Summary

Don't leave your employees in the dark about what is going on. Share information with them.

COMMANDMENT VII

LISTEN TO EMPLOYEES

"The open door policy is very important at HP because it characterizes the management style to which we are dedicated. It means managers are available, open, and receptive...It is a procedure that encourages and, in fact, ensures that the communication flow be upward as well as downward." [20]

—David Packard
Co-founder and former CEO, Hewlett-Packard

B eing a good listener is one of the key abilities of an effective manager. Listening to employees is the inverse of sharing information. When you listen to employees, your purpose is to get employees to share information with you. If you don't listen to your employees, you will miss out on key pieces of information, increase the chances of miscommunication, and run the risk that they will give up trying to communicate with you. Managers should listen to employees to get ideas about how to improve the business and to uncover problems.

Employee Suggestions

Larry Rogers is a vice president of a national non-profit organization. Last year, he took a trip to San Francisco with his wife to visit his parents. Larry also used the trip to scout hotels downtown, because he was put in charge of a team that had to find a location for the organization's annual conference the following year. During his visit, he got a tour of the conference rooms at the hotel he and his wife were staying at as well as a few of the nearby hotels. They all seemed to be pretty close in price and quality so Larry had initially decided to recommend the hotel he stayed at to the board.

However, on the morning he and his wife were leaving town, they had to get a cab from their hotel by 6:30 a.m. to make their flight. Unfortunately, Larry hit the snooze button on the hotel alarm clock. He and his wife ended up sleeping late and had to rush frantically to get out of there on time. Larry was ready first and went to the lobby to check out. After checking out, he went over to the hotel restaurant to get a cup of coffee but it was closed. He asked a bellman about the restaurant, and he said it did not open until 7 a.m.

Larry was really upset, because he is one of those people that has to have coffee every morning. The bellman empathized with him and apologized profusely. He also said that he and the other bellmen had asked the general manager on several occasions to let them make a pot of coffee for the early risers. But every time they asked the general manager he would just ignore them.

When Larry got back home, he changed his mind and recommended a neighboring hotel. His organization had the conference there the following year and the group ended up spending over $35,000 at the hotel during their stay. The simple failure to listen to the bellmen's suggestion cost that hotel dearly.

Managers should constantly be asking employees "What do you think?" Employees know more about their jobs than anyone else, but they are usually the last ones to be asked how things could be done better. Besides being experts at their jobs, employees can bring a fresh perspective to analyzing the problems of the business because they have a different set of life experiences. Collectively, they can be just as valuable as a really good consultant and the best part is that their advice is free. In addition, if you listen to employees and are open to what they have to say, then employees will be much more willing to embrace things that you ask them to do.

Listening to employees' ideas is also a tremendous morale booster. Most workers would cherish the opportunity to give input on decisions that affect their jobs. When managers listen to employees, the message being communicated to them is "You are important and we value what you have to say." That is one of the highest compliments that a manager can give an employee. My cousin used to manage a business that employed many high school students. One of his best employees once said to him, "I like coming to work here, Jeremy." Startled, my cousin asked "Why?" since the employee did not have a very enjoyable job. He responded, "Because you are the only person in my life who listens to my ideas."

When trying to get employees to give suggestions, try to withhold what your opinion is on the subject until after they tell you what they think. You should try to have an open mind about ideas that come from your employees. We all see the world in our own way, so don't immediately dismiss what your employees are saying just because it is not in accord with your line of thinking. You don't want employees just repeating what you say. Constructive, respectful debates are a sign of a healthy organization. After all, you can buy a parrot if you just want to hear your ideas repeated.

Granted, not everything your employees have to say will be useful since they may see things from a more narrow point of view. And listening to employees doesn't mean you have to agree with all of their ideas. You may have to agree to disagree. Another possibility is that you end up implementing a portion of the suggestion or modifying it a little.

However, if you never implement any of their suggestions, your employees might think "Why are they asking me for suggestions if they aren't even going to implement the good ones?" Also, if you have already made up your mind, it is better to just tell employees that you have made a decision. You should not ask employees for their opinion when you know you are not going to budge anyway.

One key point to remember is that listening to employees' ideas is not about compromising. It is about making the best decision no matter where it comes from.

If you say two plus two equals four and one of your employees says two plus two equals eight, that doesn't mean you should meet them half way and come to the conclusion that two plus two equals six.

In addition, there may come a time when you have to turn down a good suggestion even though you agree it is a good idea, because you don't have the authority to implement the change. For example, imagine a pizza restaurant has numerous complaints over the quality of sauce they use. Therefore, an employee suggests to his manager that they try out some new sauce vendors and choose one that provides a better product than the one they currently have. The manager agrees that it is a good idea, but tells the employee it can't be done because the restaurant is part of a franchise and the franchise agreement states that all of the ingredients in the pizza must be bought from the parent company.

However, even if you can't do anything about an employee's suggestion, it will make them feel good that they were able to share their idea with somebody instead of keeping it bottled up inside. And, who knows, maybe one day you will be in a position where you can do something about it.

Although there are some things that you won't be able to budge on, a lot of times there is nothing stopping a good idea from being implemented. Many outdated policies stay around for much longer than they should for no other reason than "We have always done it that way." Therefore, you are much better off having a bias leaning towards considering change rather than leaning against it. After all, employee suggestions can make your life easier by maximizing efficiency, increasing revenues, or cutting costs.

There are many ways to gather employee suggestions. You can let employees set up a time to speak with you, ask them their opinions when you are brainstorming ideas about a new project, give them an anonymous survey, encourage them to take a devil's advocate role to try to pinpoint any weaknesses in a plan, etc. At first, employees may be reluctant to give suggestions. But they will soon begin giving them when they are certain that you want to hear them. One way to help encourage employee suggestions is to praise employees for giving suggestions even if you do not put them into practice.

The key to any employee suggestion program is the genuine desire of the manager to hear the ideas that employees have and willingness to implement the good ones. That, more than anything, will determine how successful it is. If you ridicule, dismiss, or ignore all of their ideas, then you are sending the message that you are really not taking them seriously which makes it unlikely that you will get any additional ones in the future.

Here is an example that discusses one of the greatest employee suggestions:

In 1968, Dr. Spence Silver was working on trying to improve adhesives that 3M used in several of its tapes. He accidentally created an adhesive that did not stick very well to surfaces. Over the next five years, Dr. Silver spread the word inside the company through seminars and face to face conversations about the potential of the new adhesive. A new product development researcher named Art Fry attended one seminar and became very interested in the new adhesive. After he became aggravated with how his scrap paper bookmarks constantly fell out of his church choir book of hymns, Fry came up with the idea that the adhesive would make a good bookmark. Finally, after winning over the skeptics within 3M, they came up with a product that was introduced in 1980 and became 3M's Outstanding New Product the following year.

What was the product? Post-it Notes.[21]

Every time you see Post-it Notes from now on, remember that they originated from an employee suggestion.

Uncover Problems

Managers should also listen to employees to uncover problems. Employees should be able to voice concerns so managers can deal with these concerns before they become lingering problems. You don't want to have the impression that everything is going well when it's not. The reason is that the problem will have to be dealt with sometime in the future anyway so you are probably better off hearing about it now.

The process of listening to employees to uncover problems is much like periodically changing the oil in your car. If you don't change the oil, unknown problems will begin to slowly build up until that dreaded day comes when you are stuck on the side of the road after your car breaks down and you have to call a tow truck. Just as taking your car in every three thousand miles to get the oil changed will help ensure your automotive machine is in top working condition, listening to employees to uncover problems will help ensure that your human resources "machine" is in top working condition.

Therefore, you want to have an environment where employees can be honest with you about problems they are having. The best way to do this is to ask open-ended questions like "How is everything going?" Then, listen to the answers without getting outwardly upset even if what they have to say is not good news, and do what you can to remove any obstacles that are in the way of employees being able to do their jobs. However, this does not mean that you solve the normal problems that employees have in their jobs for them. This has to do with major problems or ones that are out of the control of employees. There is a fine line between micromanaging and getting involved when that is the right thing to do.

You might say, "But I have an open door management policy. Employees are free to set up a time to talk to me anytime they want." However, most employees don't think that you really want to hear what they have to say. They fear if they voice their opinions you might become upset, label them a complainer, or do nothing about it. A true open door environment is one where employees feel comfortable communicating with you how they feel.

Managers should take this whole process very seriously and not do it halfheartedly by seeming disinterested or not listening attentively. If you approach listening to employees in a phony fashion, then the employees will become upset and not communicate their true feelings to you. Your words will ring hollow if you say you have an open door policy and then constantly put off meeting with them or ignore what they are saying when they speak to you. Also, when listening to employees it is very important to keep the conversation confidential. One of the quickest ways to ruin any trust you have with your employees is to get the reputation that you will tell others what your employees have told you in private.

When listening to employees, you should first absorb what they say by letting it sink in a little before you respond. You should also listen to employees without judgment and stay neutral. Employees should be heard without the fear of being reprimanded. Managers should not "shoot the messenger" by lashing out at employees if they bring bad news. This will discourage employees from bringing bad news in the future and that is not what you want.

Once you have heard what an employee has to say, you should decide whether you need to do anything about it and ask the employee if they want you to look into the problem. However, remember that there are always two sides to every story and you are only seeing things from one person's point of view. At this point, it is best not to promise the employee anything until you have looked into the matter. Also, there are certain times when you could step in and get involved, but it would be better for the employee to take care of the problem themselves.

Even though listening to employees is important, you want to make sure that you don't allow employees to dump every little problem on you. Therefore, you should first ask the employee what they have done to solve the problem. They should take responsibility for dealing with the problem to the extent that they can.

In addition, managers should realize that being available for employees and having an open door policy does not mean that they can come into your office any time they feel like it. You must set boundaries or you might face a situation where you are constantly interrupted and can't get any of your own work done. For example, you can tell employees that if your door is closed that means that you have to be left alone. Or, if they ask to talk to you while you are out of your office but busy, you should politely say that you can't talk now and give them a time when they can talk to you. Employees understand that you can't always talk to them that moment so they should not have any problem with this.

Here are two examples that illustrate the importance of managers listening to employees to solve problems before they get out of hand:

Example #1 - Katie Morsovillo is the director of business development at a New York City retailer. She has had some problems recently with one of her employees who used to be one of her best. It all started about six months ago when Katie chose a person outside the company for the assistant director of business development position which she thought the employee wanted. Since then, the employee often arrived late to work and took extra time at lunch, but always left right on time. This person was cheerful before, but became less friendly and a bit short-tempered at work. The employee would even stay on personal calls when they needed to be taking care of important business. Katie finally decided to have a talk with the employee to see what her problem was and in doing so got everything worked out.

Example #2 - Christine Dunne is a business analyst for an East Coast women's clothing company. She is a single mother who recently got a divorce from her high school sweetheart after being separated for a while and unable to reconcile their problems. Christine loves her job since she is big into fashion and would not consider doing anything else. But her separation and divorce has really taken a toll on her. When her husband was around, he would drop their daughter off at day care every morning and pick her up in the afternoon, because it was right near where he worked on Long Island. After the separation, Christine had to take over this responsibility. This was especially difficult in the afternoons, because the day care center closed at 6:30 p.m. and it was tough to make it out there after work by that time.

In addition, her mother recently had health problems that the doctors had trouble diagnosing. Christine had to speak many times with several different doctors to try to figure out what needed to be done with her mother. She even started doing many of her chores during lunch, because that was one of the few times during the day that she had free. Christine knew the problems in her personal life were affecting her work life and she desperately wanted to talk to her manager about it. But she thought that it was best not to bring personal issues into the office. Luckily, Christine's manager called her in for a talk soon after that and she got to let her manager know what she was going through.

In the first example, Katie was shocked to find out in their talk that her employee had been having some serious personal problems over the past six months. They were the root cause of the behavior. In the second example, Christine was relieved to finally explain her divorce, daughter's day care situation, and mother's illness to her manager. They solved the problem by allowing Christine to come in to work thirty minutes later and leave thirty minutes earlier. Then, in order to make up for the time she missed during the day, Christine would do computer work at home every night for an hour after her daughter went to sleep.

These two examples show how differently someone can interpret a situation without having full knowledge of what is going on. Katie is Christine's manager.

The truth is that Christine had no desire to get the assistant director of business development position. She was perfectly happy in her job. The change in behavior had nothing to do with that and everything to do with her personal problems. She was not on the phone talking to friends. She was on the phone talking to doctors.

Christine was often late but always leaving right on time to deal with the day care situation. She was taking long lunches to get as many of her chores done as possible. And Christine was less friendly and a bit short-tempered due to the stress of the divorce combined with her mother's health, not because she was bitter about not landing that position.

The point of this example is not to assign blame. Frankly, Christine should have said something to her manager on her own long before six months had passed. However, if Katie had always been in the habit of listening to Christine to uncover any problems with her job, then this matter would not have drawn-out six months either. A lot of times what you assume will be correct, but sometimes you are just looking at the tip of the iceberg.

Summary

Knowledge is power. Listen to employees to get suggestions and uncover problems.

COMMANDMENT VIII

MANAGE EACH
EMPLOYEE DIFFERENTLY

*"We are all different. A good manager will
recognize those differences and treat each person
as an individual."* [22]

—Mary Kay Ash
Founder and former CEO, Mary Kay Cosmetics

A couple of months ago I bought a new suit. After
I selected the one I wanted, I had to get my
measurements taken. They measured my waist.
They measured my arms. They measured my legs. They
measured around my chest. It seemed like it took longer
to take my measurements than it did to select the suit!
This was time well spent, though. Can you imagine if
stores only sold suits in one size? It's not enough to buy
a nice suit. It must fit well, too.

In the same sense, you should tailor your management style to the needs and abilities of each individual
employee. Although general rules certainly apply, you
should not manage employees with the cookie cutter con-

cept of dealing with them all the same way. In addition, trying to change people is futile because people are who they are. The best strategy is to take a customized approach with each employee in order to make them as productive as they can be.

All Employees Are Unique

Employees have different abilities, needs, and preferences. Some people want to grow and have their responsibilities increased so they constantly have a new challenge. Others are perfectly content doing the same job year after year. Some employees don't want you to help them at all. Others need a little more guidance. Some workers like to be praised in public. Others are totally uncomfortable with it. Some people want the corner office and a lofty title. Others could care less about status symbols. Some employees like to start work early in the morning so they can leave earlier. Others like to start later in the morning and then be the one who turns out the lights when they leave. Some workers would love to sit in on a management meeting. Others don't want to have anything to do with them. Some people want to network with employees from other departments. Others only want to deal with people in their own area. Some employees get a boost of energy from working on a team. Others just want to work alone.

Some workers are quick learners, but once they get the process down they get bored. Others are slow learners, but love the monotony once they nail down the steps involved. Some people like to be creative in finding solutions to a problem. Others want you to give them more structure and feedback. Some employees are good at thinking of ideas, but not implementing them. Others don't have many good ideas, but can implement the ideas that other people suggest. Some workers are happy to work overtime. Others have absolutely no desire to work over forty hours per week. Some people need to be constantly told that they are doing a good job. Others only want to be rewarded with the opportunity to do stimulating work. Some employees are too shy to give their ideas in front of a group, preferring to tell you in private. Others have no problem voicing their opinion in front of everybody else. Some workers will complain at the drop of a hat. Others will never complain. Some people will be more productive working on a team with John, Fred, and Terri. Others will be most effective when they work with Alexa, Judy, and Matt.

What Employees Want From Their Manager

Recently, I asked ten people the question "What do you want most from your manager to help you succeed in your job?" Here are their answers:

Employee #1 - "I want my manager to teach me exactly what I need to know to do my job. I'd like to know a lot more than just the basics, because I don't want to have to figure out everything on my own. Also, if I ever have a question, I want my manager to be available to answer it."

Employee #2 - "I really want my manager to give me additional responsibilities as a reward for doing a good job. My juices really get flowing when I begin a new challenge."

Employee #3 - "The most important thing to me is that I want to know where I stand. If I am doing a great job, let me know. If I am doing a lousy job, let me know. It just bugs the heck out of me when my manager does not give me any feedback on my job performance."

Employee #4 - "My favorite aspect of my job is being able to work with other talented people on team projects. Most of the time, they work out really well. But sometimes I get stuck on a team with a major slacker. That is the easiest way to take the wind out of my sails. The rest of us will be working hard and one person won't contribute anything. Above all, I want my manager to do something with these people. Frankly, I could care less if they are fired or not. Just don't make me work with them."

Employee #5 - "I am pretty ambitious so I want my manager to be my mentor and show me the ropes. I would like to go out to lunch with my manager every once in a while and talk about the ins and outs of the business. It would also be nice to be introduced to other important managers in the company."

Employee #6 - "I want my manager to allow me to be creative in coming up with solutions to problems. It seems like some managers talk about 'thinking outside the box', but when push comes to shove things usually have to be done their way. That makes work a lot less interesting."

Employee #7 - "Above all, I want to have an open line of communication with my manager. Every once in a while, I need to vent about a customer or another employee. And it is nice when I can go to my manager with a problem I am having and know I will be heard."

Employee #8 - "I really can't stand managers that are bossy and critical. Constant negativity really brings me down. I would like my manager to do things to lift me up."

Employee #9 - "I will probably come off sounding like a loner and maybe I am. But what I want most is to be left alone to do my job."

Employee #10 - "I want my manager to respect me as a person, not just see me as another employee number. I know respect has to be earned. But if I've earned it, then give it to me."

The diversity of these answers is fascinating. They illustrate the different needs that all employees have. Therefore, you should get to know your employees, learn what makes each of them tick, and then adjust how you manage them accordingly.

Examples

Here are four examples regarding effectively adapting to employees to maximize their productivity:

John Sedbrook is the director of information systems for a consumer electronics company. After the retirement of one of his project managers, he promoted a very bright young programmer to replace him. The new project manager did pretty well in the position for a year and a half. But one day he came into John's office and confessed that his duties as a manager really wore him down. The new project manager admitted he liked the pay and status of the new position, but he realized that wasn't what was most important to him and requested to go back to being a programmer. John granted his request and gave him a lateral move to a senior programmer position. He then promoted one of the experienced programmers who was not the most technically proficient one in the group, but would be good at handling the managerial duties of the job.

The software development division of a Northern California based software company gives employees some flexibility to choose what hours they work. Although there are certain times when the developers have to be there for a meeting, the developers can arrive anywhere from 7 a.m. to 11 a.m. and with a one hour lunch they can leave anywhere from 4 p.m. to 8 p.m. depending on what time they arrive in the morning.

There are a few who are early risers and make it to work by 7 a.m. every day. Others prefer to start work later in the day.

Sometimes, if the developers have something going on outside of work during work hours, they will arrive to work early, go do something else, and then come back in the evening to complete a day's worth of work. One employee who usually starts late does this once a week in the spring so he can attend his daughter's soccer practices in the middle of the afternoon.

The developers love the flexible schedule format, because it allows them to work when they are the most productive. Granted, this obviously would not be possible in a retail or manufacturing environment, because in these types of businesses you have to be there at a certain time. But it has worked very well for the software company, because most of the time it doesn't matter what time the developers are at the office as long as they are getting their work done.

Jessica Donohue is a district manager for a national fitness chain. Twice a year, she meets with the manager from each gym in her district to go over their performance. Most of the managers have been very cooperative in these meetings. However, one of them, Carl Griffin, was always a headache for Jessica. Carl was always pleasant when Jessica praised his work. But he would get very defensive whenever she would bring up areas where he needed to improve. After going through three performance reviews without making any progress, Jessica gave up on her conventional tactics and decided to take an unorthodox approach.

During the fourth meeting, Jessica told Carl that from then on he was going to be responsible for his own performance review. They would still meet every six months, but Carl would be responsible for judging his performance and he would communicate the results to

Jessica. Surprisingly, this ended up working like a charm. Carl was much tougher on himself than Jessica ever was and tried hard to improve in areas where he needed to get better. Much to Jessica's delight, the self-evaluation seemed to get Carl to take ownership of making the necessary improvements.

Tom Stenmark manages a technical support call-in center for an internet service provider. He was promoted to the position after three years of being in a tech support position. Tom now manages twelve tech support employees. One of them, Danny, can diagnose and solve problems that customers have better than anybody in the department including Tom. However, he does not have very good social skills and often came off as obnoxious and patronizing when speaking to customers. That led to a lot of complaints which put Danny in jeopardy of losing his job.

Tom was in a bind because he did not want to lose an employee who knew so much. Also, almost all of the people in tech support were entry-level employees who were there to get some experience before moving on to another position in the company. As a result, Tom was always stuck with a few employees who were not very good at their jobs due to their inexperience. However, Danny preferred to work in tech support and had no desire to leave the department. Even though Tom wanted to keep him, he could not accept having customers being treated disrespectfully.

Tom came up with the idea of creating a new position for Danny. Instead of dealing with customers directly, he would assist any of the other tech support employees when they encountered a problem that they could not immediately solve for the customer. Usually, when one of the new employees had a question, they would try to ask another person in tech support, but that was not always possible if everybody was on a call. As a result, Tom would often get interrupted by them when they would have to come to him to ask questions. But with Danny in his new position, Tom was rarely taken away from the other responsibilities of his job.

The tech support employees also liked the arrangement. They said they felt guilty in the past when they had to ask Tom a question, because they knew he was busy. In addition, they understood it was just Danny being Danny when he got a little obnoxious and they did not take it personally.

Summary

In regard to the Model T his company introduced early in the 20th century, Henry Ford said that customers could have the car in any color they wanted as long as it was black. With your employees, you will need to offer a little more customized approach to make them as productive as possible.

COMMANDMENT IX

CONFRONT UNPRODUCTIVE BEHAVIOR

"A team will perform well only if peak performance is elicited from the individuals in it." [23]

—**Andrew Grove**
Co-founder and former CEO, Intel

At some point, employee performance will falter. An employee may start coming in to work late every day. Or the monthly reports will be completed one or two days late. Or a rift occurs between two employees who used to get along. These types of things are going to happen with employees. When they do, your job is to help fix the problem.

Confronting unproductive behavior is like stopping the spreading of a disease. Once there is a problem, it is unlikely that it will solve itself. Usually, what ends up happening is that the problem gets worse. Most big problems start as little ones. Therefore, you have the choice of dealing with the problem as it exists now or dealing with a worse problem later.

Confronting Problems is Not Fun, But Necessary

Dealing with underperforming employees is typically one of the most unpleasant parts of your job as a manager. Even though it is uncomfortable for most managers to confront employees, you should not feel guilty about bringing poor performers up to an acceptable standard. After all, it's nothing personal. You are just doing your job.

However, it is very easy to put off dealing with a people problem. But agonizing over confronting the problem with the employee is often worse than the confrontation itself. And the longer you wait to address a problem, the more built up frustration and anger you will have inside you.

Managers do not confront unproductive behavior for many reasons. These include: not wanting to look like the bad guy; being afraid of making the employee upset; knowing it will be very uncomfortable for both parties; being worried about ruining a friendship; not wanting the employee to quit and have to go through the hiring process again; being scared the employee might turn the table and bring up a list of the manager's downfalls; not wanting to hurt the employee's feelings; fearing that the employee may try to undermine their authority, etc.

Even though you may not want to hurt employees by pointing out things that need to be corrected, you will hurt them more by not addressing the problem. An employee who performs poorly is hurt because deep down they usually know they are not doing a good job. By not confronting unproductive behavior, you are allowing them to be mediocre. This does employees a great disservice by robbing them of the pride they would have by doing a good job. By dealing with the problem, you are eliminating a roadblock in the employee's progression.

In addition, you owe it to yourself to not have to put up with unproductive behavior. If you are constantly stressed out about an employee, your own work is going to suffer. Though confronting problems can initially be a little uncomfortable, you will be rewarded with the relief of no longer having that monkey on your back. Also, if you correct unproductive behavior early on, you will be more likely to have employees who act right in the future, because they know you will hold them accountable for their behavior.

Addressing the Employee About the Problem

When confronting problems, you have to pick your battles. You don't want to major in minor things. With some minor infractions, you are better off letting them slide. Morale will sink and trust will weaken if employees think you are always trying to find them doing something wrong. Also, if you punish employees for making a mistake when they were genuinely trying to do their best, they will really begin to doubt themselves which will end up making them less productive. Making mistakes every once in a while should be expected from all employees. But constantly making mistakes is a whole different matter and this is where you must step in and do something.

Once you have decided to address the problem, you should choose a time and location to meet with the employee so you will not be interrupted. If you allow yourself to be distracted, you are minimizing the importance of the meeting. Also, be sure to meet with the employee when you are at least in a reasonably good mood. If you are in a bad mood, you will be more likely to lash out at the employee and the meeting will not be productive. You should also try to make sure that the employee is not upset when you meet to confront their behavior.

In addition, you should not confront an employee about unproductive behavior in front of other employees. If you do this, you are blatantly disrespecting the employee. This will destroy employee morale because you are creating an environment where employees fear you. Other employees will then wonder if that will happen to them next and productivity will suffer as a result.

For example, if an employee is constantly late for meetings, don't give him a tongue lashing in front of everybody else when he arrives. Even though the behavior needs to be confronted, you need to do it without having a negative effect on the other employees. The best case scenario is for you to correct the behavior without rocking the boat. Therefore, you should do your best to make sure that none of your other employees even knows that you are confronting the employee. Employees will really appreciate it if you allow them to retain their dignity when you are correcting their behavior.

Also, just because an employee needs their behavior corrected does not mean that you can say anything to them. Managers should not meet with the employee to vent at them. This may make you feel better, but it will only worsen the problem. You should keep in mind that your goal is to improve the behavior of the employee. At this point, the more positive communication you have with the employee, the more likely you are to get the employee to change their behavior in the way that you want.

In addition, managers should know that just because unproductive behavior is confronted does not mean that the overall situation will improve. Consider this example:

A regional manager of an office supply distributor was very upset over employees taking more than an hour for their lunch breaks. The office policy was that employees could take an hour break anywhere between 11:30 a.m. and 1:30 p.m. The problem was that few employees would ever be in the office during that two hour period. For example, employees would leave at 11:30 a.m. and come back at 1:00 p.m. Then, another day they might leave at noon and come back at 1:20 p.m.

The regional manager was often out of the office so for a long time he did not have any idea this was going on. But when he figured it out, he was furious. As a result, one day after that he went out to the parking lot right before 11:30 a.m. with a box of 3" by 5" cards. On each one, he had written "You must be back from lunch by." Then, when each employee left for lunch, he wrote down the time they needed to be back by and handed it to them. For example, if an employee left at 11:45 a.m., he would write down 12:45 p.m. on the card.

Needless to say, the move was quite a shock to all of the employees. Every one of them got back well within an hour that day and every day after that. On the surface, the regional manager accomplished his objective of eliminating the abuse of lunch breaks by employees. But within two weeks, five out of twenty one employees in the regional office quit without turning in any notice. In addition, morale immediately went from being a little below average to nonexistent. The regional manager ended up getting fired three months later because of the horrendous performance in his region. Even though he was totally right to take action, the regional manager clearly did not fix the problem in the correct manner. He won the battle but lost the war.

When confronting a problem, you should communicate how you see the problem from your point of view and explain why the behavior must change. This includes discussing the negative impact that it is having on other employees. Also, be sure to focus on the behavior and don't attack the employee. You want to communicate that you care about and respect the employee as a person, but their behavior needs to change. In addition, focus on what the employee needs to do in the future to fix the problem by clearly explaining what you want done differently. You should not dwell too much on all of the instances in the past where the employee acted incorrectly.

You should also do your best to only correct behavior you have seen. If you don't have hard facts, you risk splitting hairs over your and their perceptions of the situation. In addition, specific examples of the unproductive behavior should be provided. Instead of saying "You are late to work all of the time", you should say "You were at least thirty minutes late this past Monday, Tuesday, and Thursday."

When meeting with the employee, you will be most effective if you focus on one problem at a time. You don't want to dump too much on an employee at once. Can you imagine saying "You are constantly taking two hour lunches, impolite to some of the other employees, and charging too much to the company credit card. Where should we start?" This will overload the employee and they will probably get defensive which won't solve anything. Also, it is best to confront unproductive behavior as soon as you can after it has happened. Employees will tend to tune out if it has been a long time since the behavior has occurred.

Managers should know that some employees who are underperforming genuinely have no clue that they aren't doing a good job. You might be ready to pull your hair out, because they are constantly doing things wrong. But you have to tell them so you are sure they know, because giving out subtle hints is not good enough. A lot of times employees are fired and when they are told the reasons they claim that they had no idea that their manager felt that way.

When you talk to employees, you should first give them a chance to explain the reason for their behavior. They may come straight out and admit that they have not done a good job and need to improve. Or, they may reveal a hidden frustration that has been eating them up inside. It is also possible that there could be a valid reason why an employee's performance level is not where it should be. One legitimate reason might be that the employee has not received enough training. That is why it is best to let employees try to explain themselves before you jump to conclusions. Employees will often blame their co-workers for problems and you will have to decide whether or not what they are saying is true. However, keep in mind that some employees can be very innovative in coming up with excuses. At some point, you have to say enough is enough.

Once you have determined that the employee's behavior needs to change, you must decide how the problem will be fixed. Although you probably have some ideas, you should also solicit suggestions from the employee. When they are involved in deciding what to do, employees will usually be more open to fixing the problem. Once an employee gives some ideas about solving the problem, you should weigh the benefits of each one and determine which ones are feasible. Then, you and the employee should come to an agreement about what specific course of action the employee is going to take. At that point, the employee is responsible for correcting the behavior.

Once you have addressed the problem with the

employee, it is important that you monitor the situation to make sure the problem is fixed. If the problem persists and you have another meeting with the employee, you will have to work with them to figure out a new strategy since the original one did not work. At this point, you can't accept the same answer as the first time because the problem did not get solved. You should also let the employee know that if things don't change soon they run the risk of being terminated. Employees should know exactly what the consequences will be if their behavior does not change.

Summary

Unproductive behavior must be tactfully confronted. If not, the problem will only get worse.

COMMANDMENT X

REPLACE UNPRODUCTIVE EMPLOYEES

"Removing people will always be the hardest decision a leader faces. Anyone who 'enjoys doing it' shouldn't be on the payroll, and neither should anyone who 'can't do it.'" [24]

—Jack Welch
Former CEO, General Electric

Probably the most unpleasant part of a manager's job is firing employees. Even when a worker deserves to be fired, most managers will feel very uncomfortable when they break the news to them and guilty for putting somebody on the unemployment line. It is usually difficult to say goodbye even if you are not crazy about the employee. I once witnessed a grizzled old veteran mutter to himself "I need a scotch" after he had to fire several employees. Nevertheless, keeping unproductive employees around or delaying what is inevitable will not solve any problems. At some point, you have to cut your losses.

Reasons for Firing Unproductive Employees

Numerous problems will occur if habitually unproductive employees are not replaced. As previously mentioned, if you tolerate mediocre employees, then you are tolerating giving your customers a mediocre product. That alone should scare you into replacing poor performers. Also, low employee morale will creep in if these employees are kept around, because productive employees will end up subsidizing the unproductive ones to make sure that everything gets done. Good workers will soon become bitter because they have to shoulder too much of the workload. If the situation persists, you run the risk that the productive employees will quit working hard or leave for another company.

Often times, an employee who gets fired realizes later on that it was a blessing in disguise. It can force people to take a hard look at their lives which can be very beneficial.

For example, Gerald is a friend of mine who had worked as an accountant for fourteen years. Two years ago, he was fired from his accounting firm because he was not performing adequately. He had been employed with the company for eight years and they gave him every chance to bounce back after his performance began to slip. But he never managed to get himself back on track.

The truth is Gerald never wanted to be an accountant. Because his dad was an accountant and his grandfather was a bookkeeper, Gerald was sort of expected to pursue accounting. Therefore, he got a degree in accounting and later became a CPA. The money he earned was good and his family was happy with his career, but Gerald was never content being an accountant. Privately, he had always dreamed of starting his own graphic design business. Gerald had incredible artistic talent and loved to draw and paint in his free time. It seemed to serve as a release from what he felt was a boring accounting job.

After Gerald was fired, he decided to use the severance pay to start the graphic design business. After just two years, he now has more demand for his work than he can handle. But he loves every minute of it. Recently, he told me that getting fired was the best thing that ever happened to him. Even though he was a little bitter at the time, looking back on it he knew he was not doing a good job and was not being fair to the people he worked with. It made him re-evaluate what he really wanted out of life and provided the kick start he needed to make the leap.

Steps to Take Before Firing an Employee

There are times when an employee should be fired immediately. These can include when an employee blatantly disregards authority, gets into a physical altercation with another employee, verbally abuses a customer, or steals from the company. In these types of cases, the employee does not deserve another chance to correct their behavior. However, as previously mentioned, under normal circumstances when employees are not productive you should first communicate to them that their behavior needs to change and give them a chance to get better.

Unfortunately, more often than not, your efforts to improve an unproductive employee's performance will only result in a relatively small, short-term improvement. If you have given an employee a sufficient opportunity to change their behavior and they fail to do so, then you have no other choice but to replace them. In a sense, you are letting employees fire themselves. After having a chance to keep their job, they have blown the opportunity. This will relieve a lot of the guilt that you might have.

When employees are struggling, managers should also think about whether or not they are doing work that fits their strengths. If the employee can't succeed in their current job, consider changing their duties or discussing with other managers in your company if they could use the employee in their department. Sometimes a worker just needs to be doing a different type of work in order to be more productive.

Imagine you are playing golf and you have to choose a club for three shots. The shots are a ten foot putt, a forty yard chip shot, and a drive off of the tee of a par five. In your bag, you have a driver, a pitching wedge, and a putter. Which club are you going to use for each shot? Let's say you decide to use the pitching wedge for the ten foot putt, the driver for the forty yard chip shot, and the putter for the drive off of the tee of the par five.

That would be the perfect recipe for disaster on the golf course, because you are obviously choosing the wrong club for each shot. The putter is designed for putts, the pitching wedge is designed for chip shots, and the driver is designed for long drives. The right club needs to be used to make sure that you are giving yourself the best chance to hit a good shot in each situation.

The same is true with the type of work you give employees. You have to know what they are good at so you can put them in a position where they will succeed.

For example, Dr. Don Kelleher is a research scientist at one of the top pharmaceutical companies. He describes how he took an employee that was not working out in another group and made him a productive member of his group:

"One of the related research teams in our division hired a guy a couple of years ago to work with their team. I saw some of his work and this guy, and I do not use the term lightly, was a borderline genius. The problem was that he was very self-centered and tended to talk about himself a lot. It wasn't malicious or anything, that's just the way he was. Unfortunately, the scientists that he worked with did not like him because of this. Plus, they had him doing work that was well below his level and he did not like it at all since his talent was being wasted.

"This went on for almost a year and a half before they were finally about to fire him. When I heard that was going to happen, I suggested that he come work for me and they were happy to accommodate my request. I was working on three or four projects and needed to delegate some work. So I gave him complete control of one of them that I knew he would excel at. Frankly, he was so good in that particular area of research that he did a much better job than I would have. All I had to do was give him a little bit of guidance and then let him do his thing. He loved it because he got to do work he really enjoyed and felt his talents were being fully utilized."

Costs of Employee Turnover

Even though it is a good idea to replace unproductive employees, managers should realize that it comes with a price tag. The following list shows how many hidden costs there are every time an employee is replaced.

The financial impact of employee turnover can include the cost of:

◆ Advertising for the position

◆ Looking through resumes

◆ Interviewing for the position

◆ Background checks

◆ Drug tests

◆ Referral bonuses

◆ Relocation expenses

◆ Setting up an employee's e-mail account and passwords for company software

◆ Getting a security badge

◆ Processing the paperwork for a departing and arriving employee

◆ Training the new employee

◆ Lost productivity and decreased customer satisfaction while the new employee learns the job

High turnover can also be a real strain on managers, because it immediately translates into a larger workload. Before an employee is hired, a fair amount of time is spent getting the word out about the position and interviewing candidates. However, that is usually the easy part compared to the time it takes to train the employee in their new position. Initially, you have to drop everything you are doing and spend enough time with the employee to even get them up to a working level of competency. As a result, the quality of your own work will likely suffer because you do not have as much time to attend to it. Even when the employee can operate reasonably well on their own, they will still have to interrupt you with questions that come up that have not been answered yet. And if you cut corners by inadequately training them, then employees will inevitably get frustrated. This will increase the possibility that they might not stay long.

Current employees also suffer with high employee turnover. They are usually left to pick up the slack before the position is filled and while the new employee is being trained. When high employee turnover is persistent, current employees are susceptible to getting burned out. They might start to complain to you about the increased difficulty of being able to do their own jobs and may even leave because of it. If this happens, your best employees are likely to leave first, because they probably have plenty of other options. Then, you may start to worry about keeping them which will stress you out even more.

As you can see, high employee turnover can create a vicious cycle and this is a problem that you can do without. This is not to say that you want employee turnover to be zero. You want good employees to be moving up and you also should be replacing unproductive employees with much better ones. And if you have the same staff for years and years, things are likely to get a little stale. The point is the managerial duties associated with a low level of employee turnover will likely fit comfortably into your workload. The key is to not let employee turnover get out of control, because when that happens you are really going to be in trouble.

Firing the Employee

Once you have decided to fire an employee, you should take certain steps. The most important is to make sure you are following all employment laws and document that you are doing so. If you don't, you will expose yourself to lawsuits. Also, you should not go back on your decision. The employee may plead to stay. But if their behavior has not changed after repeated attempts to correct it, there is no reason to think that things will be different this time.

In addition, you should not let other employees outside of human resources know that you are about to fire the employee. If you do, the information has a good chance of getting back to the employee. They should never have to hear through the grapevine that they are about to be fired. Also, any employee with a heart will feel terrible about being around a co-worker who is about to be fired, even if it is deserved.

You should also treat the individual with respect. Tell

them privately that they are being fired and keep all discussions confidential. Besides being the right thing to do, this will make sure that the disruption to other employees is minimal. In addition, you should remain totally calm no matter how the employee reacts to the news of being fired.

Once the employee is gone, you should not criticize them and rub their name into the ground. You should only express regret that things did not work out, move on, and forget about the past. The act of firing an employee is such a strong statement that you have nothing to gain by pushing the issue further. When you gracefully fire an employee, you are showing all of your employees how much class you have. This will make them have even more respect for you.

The final and most important step is to find a suitable replacement. If you do not hire a good replacement, then you will likely have to repeat the same miserable process in the not so distant future. Even though replacing poor performers is a good idea, it is clear that the best time to do it is before they are even hired. When extra resources are invested in the hiring process to get the right person for the job, a lot of problems will be solved before they occur. For advice on that, see Commandment I…

CONCLUSION

Now that you have finished the book, what should you do now? The key is to put these ideas into practice. Obviously, this will require a lot of work. However, the benefits of having a highly productive workforce will make it all worthwhile.

Being a manager is one of the toughest jobs. The range of skill the position demands at various times is immense. To be successful, managers have to use both hard and soft approaches depending on the particular situation. Good management practices are not all "touchy feely." Below the surface, there is also a hard-nosed discipline to effective managers.

Some managers are very skilled at the hard approach. They do not tolerate slackers and have the conviction to replace employees when absolutely necessary. However, they may not be comfortable hearing employee suggestions or issuing instructions in a respectful manner. On the other hand, some managers are very skilled at the softer side of management. They are adept at praising good work or listening to a problem an employee has, but they may have trouble laying down the law. Of course, not all managers clearly fit into one of these two categories. Though, if you do, then at least you are aware of which areas are more difficult for you so you can focus on improving them.

Another reason the role of managing employees is so difficult is because it can be a thankless job. A lot of good management techniques require you to place a lot of positive attention on your employees and take it away from yourself. Sometimes you will just have to be happy to look in the mirror and know that a good job has been done, regardless of whether somebody else recognizes it or not.

Since you likely have a manager yourself, there will be times when you will not have the power to do everything you want. For example, you may not be able to hire who you want if the prospective employee demands a salary that your manager believes is too high. Even though you may be right to want to spend a little more for your top candidate, you will have to settle on somebody else. In addition, replacing unproductive employees can be very difficult to do in certain situations. However, when your choices are limited, just do the best you can with the resources and authority you have been given. That is all you can ever ask of yourself.

In conclusion, I would like to thank you for taking the time to let me share my thoughts with you. I hope your effectiveness as a manager will improve as a result of this book.

NOTES

1. Morita, Akio, *Made in Japan: Akio Morita and Sony* (New York: E.P. Dutton, 1986), p. 131.

2. "Chief Executive of the Year: Herbert D. Kelleher," *Chief Executive*, [On-line] Available: http://www.chiefexecutive.net/mag/146/article1.htm, 1999.

3. Carbonara, Peter, "Hire for Attitude, Train for Skill," Fast Company, [On-line] Available: http://www.fastcompany.com/online/04/hiring.html, August/September 1996.

4. Schultz, Howard, *Pour Your Heart Into It: How Starbucks Built a Company One Cup at a Time* (New York: Hyperion, 1997), p. 250.

5. Ibid., pp. 250-251.

6. Gruner, Stephanie L., "Lasting Impressions," *Inc.com*, [On-line] Available: http://www.inc.com/magazine/19980701/968.html, July 1, 1998.

7. Mackay, Harvey, *Swim with the Sharks Without Being Eaten Alive: Outsell, Outmanage, Outmotivate, and Outnegotiate Your Competition* (New York: Ballantine Books, 1988), p. 131.

8. Spector, Robert and McCarthy, Patrick D., *The Nordstrom Way: The Inside Story of America's #1 Customer Service Company* (New York: John Wiley & Sons, 1995), p. 98.

9. Ibid., p. 102.

10. Ibid., p. 103.

11. Richardson, Shasha. <shasha.richardson@nordstrom.com> "Nordstrom employee manual." 11 Jun. 2003. Personal e-mail.

12. Getty, J. Paul, *How to be Rich: His Formulas* (New York: Jove Books, 1965), p. 80.

13. Walton, Sam, *Sam Walton: Made in America* (New York: Bantam Books, 1992), pp. 315-316.

14. Dell, Michael, *Direct from Dell: Strategies That Revolutionized an Industry* (New York: HarperCollins Publishers, 1999), p. 131.

15. Stack, Jack with Burlingham, Bo, *The Great Game of Business* (New York: Currency Doubleday, 1992), p. 1.

16. Ibid., p. 72.

17. Ibid., p. 176.

18. Ibid., p. 178.

19. Ibid., pp. 3-4.

20. Packard, David, *The HP Way: How Bill Hewlett and I Built Our Company* (New York: HarperCollins Publishers, 1995), p. 158.

21. "Art Fry and the invention of Post-it Notes," [On-line] Available: http://www.3m.com/about3m/pioneers/fry.jhtml.

22. Ash, Mary Kay, *Mary Kay on People Management* (New York: Warner Books, 1984), p. 133.

22. Grove, Andrew, *High Output Management* (New York: Vintage Books, 1995), p. xvi.

24. Welch, Jack, *Jack: Straight from the Gut* (New York: Warner Books, 2001), p. 128.

Author's note: The names and situations in many of the examples in the book have been hidden or changed to protect certain individuals and organizations involved.

CONTACT INFORMATION

If you would like to contact the author, you are encouraged to send an e-mail to: gregblencoe@yahoo.com.